Dead Burying the Dead Under a Quaking Aspen

Poems

David Cranmer

Cover images from Adobe Stock; Design by dMix.

ISBN: 978-1-943035-34-2

www.beattoapulp.com

Dedicated to my wife, Denise, and our daughter, Ava Elyse,
who give me reason to believe, and, as always, to
Kyle J. Knapp whose imagination and vision
continues to inspire.

Table of Contents

Acknowledgments

Thank you first and foremost to Stephen J. Golds whose energy and undying support made this collection possible.

To the webzine editors who first published my poems: Gerald So, Rusty Barnes, Heather Sullivan, B F Jones, Stephen J. Golds, and Paul D. Brazill.

The best kind of poetry holds up a lens to life. David Cranmer's work goes a step further by holding up a telescopic photography lens and takes pure shots of the human condition, capturing moments in unadulterated honesty.

The poem that first brought Cranmer to my attention was "The Inconsiderate," originally published at Live Nude Poems. While reading the lines, I imagined Cranmer as a war photographer, capturing the heart-wrenching, daily anguish of people in war-torn locales and the casual cruelty of those who have long ago become acclimatized to suffering.

> Two MPs stoop by the corpse, and strike a pose
> A souvenir picture is snapped while nearby
> Cordoned off with onlookers, a woman cries.

The way Cranmer expresses so much in so few words is Carver-esque.

No one and nothing is safe from Cranmer's highly observant gaze. Including, and especially, himself. He lays himself bare in his poems, sharing the darkness and insecurities in such a way as to be endearing and at the same time wholly relatable. Take, for just one example, "Alone (after Kyle J. Knapp)," a beautiful poem dedicated to his departed nephew.

Drunken, / Inconsolable, / Tired. /
Every night / Muddled speech / Visions / And other
graceless vexations. / Myself, trying to sleep / One day /
I will.

Cranmer is able to communicate so much loss and heartache in so few lines, it leaves the reader momentarily breathless and going back to the start of the poem to read it again and again. Each poem needs to be contemplated over to truly see the attention to detail and craft.

Poetry has become somewhat dry and dusty, difficult to read, difficult to relate to as of late. However, David Cranmer has arrived to pull poetry back to where it belongs. In the hands of outsiders, outliers and those that kick back against the prigs.

I hope David continues to write poetry for as long as I'm able to read.

—*Stephen J. Golds*

Dead Burying the Dead
Under a Quaking Aspen

I've noticed again and again that it is poetry, and poetry alone, that can face death on anything like equal terms. —*Martin Amis*

On a dirt road threading out of Port-au-Prince
A man discarded alongside the ditch
By thugs, former Tonton Macoute,
Laid flat with machete hacks
Bits of bone and brain fan out from the wound
Blood seeping into the dry, dusty ground.

Our squad arrives securing the scene,
Interviewing witnesses and recording the crime
Two MPs stoop by the corpse, and strike a pose
A souvenir picture is snapped while nearby
Cordoned off with onlookers, a woman cries.

Étienne, our assigned interpreter, tells the GIs
The weeping woman is mother to the deceased
But they do not flinch—it is lost on them
How they are treating her son's remains
Like the trophy hunters of some big game.

Years on, these soldiers would be dead too,
But that day in Haiti, it was going well for them.

Talk
Small talk
Surface talk
"How's the weather?"
"What a sweet baby!"
"Nice to see you again!"
Temporary exchanges
Signifying little to nil
Just daily superfluous asides
Make up a shared human experience

Make for a distinct human misery
For those who find socializing hard
Talk equals emotional dread
No line for a common thread
Riding the slow train to
Pull the right words but
Falling short and
Left wanting
To fade
Out.

Cri de Coeur

It lives where I buried it,
there in the shadows,
where misery dwells,
and clings to life like a disease
reaching out to take my hand,
asking to be   familiar again.

And it shifts and it twists
and it pleads, and
though I know I shouldn't bend,
I owe it a few minutes
for the suffering I've caused
in creating it   I listen

to disembodied words balloon
from moldering, visceral depths.

When I've given it its due,
I beg forgiveness,
and leave before it claims dominion.
Mind control is all I have to quiet
the clawing and screaming that
echo against my receding footfalls.

He can
no longer
reconcile
the man
who smiles
at work
proactively
moving the
day forward
with
the one
who sits
at night
nursing a
scotch
& soda
lamenting
the passing
of time.

They sit,
rotting.
Vacant eyes,
not yet dead,
far from alive.
Downcast, lost
creatures
glued in spot,
like flies stuck
to a sticky trap,
but without
the buzzing
there's not
the slightest
glimpse of life
remaining.

Man, head in his lap, outside my hotel
window, healing in the Denver sun.
Oblivious, as life bores around him,
he frequently scratches both arms.
I don't get his poison, I'm a whiskey drinker
myself, but I get blown apart.

Pouring morning coffee, I keep an eye
out, making sure no one flips him for
his sneakers, watch, or a few bucks.
As a security specialist, paranoia is my
natural state, the dull cloak I wear.
He's zeroing out as I'm ironing a shirt.

By the designer threads he's wearing,
I'm guessing it's heroin. His spiral may
have him on meth, but his face doesn't
look all that fucked up   yet.
When he lifts his head, he reminds me
of a younger, ultra-slim Warren Oates.

Three quarters of an hour pass and
Slim finally traipses off, I assume to the room
where I've seen him go a handful
of times before. Soon after, I head to
my gig off Inverness West. Guarding an
empty office of universal grey and beige.

The sun that peeled the toxins from
Slim's skin pours in the window down
the wall and onto the floor, stretching

shadows across the room onto my
shoes. I type words into my iPhone,
capturing the poetry of a slow death.

Adrift between stars,
light years from nowhere,
powered down, a
voyager, in an icy cloud.

Forces want to break free—
contract—how much
of our lives do we make,
how much is circumstance?

And so on and so forth, yes,
I'm just the latest in the curse and
mark of Cain, controlled by others,
and remotely shut off.

Desperate, Erica F looks west
As Horses Head spills out
A familiar face offers her a ride
Somewhere, anywhere.

She longs to be with her children
Traveling over Mackinaw Bridge
Showing them her once home in Michigan
The driver takes her away, anywhere but there.

Last seen in Middleburgh, New York
Wanting for a brand-new day
"She feared for her life," a brother claims
A "victim of foul play," the police say.

A hole in the sky opens the divide
An endless river of restless dead
To those who aren't afforded sleep
Justice moves their way … on the creep.

Beneath floorboards, and from the dirt
A mother's bleeding heart is heard
"Every nook and cranny has its tears."
What was lost shall be restored.

Hugh Chaffin

A skilled green thumb, with weathered
caring hands and earth-crusted fingernails
is hunched over, tending his gladiolus-filled acreage.

Neighbors see him among tall, color-studded stalks
of purple, red, white, and yellow—dazzling and swaying
as he prunes and weeds the days along.

But evil slides at bent angles, unnoticed in the light
—a hitcher invited in for respite delivers no mercy,
and behind shuttered windows, strikes.

"This doesn't happen here?" a village pines in shock,
learning a fellow resident had been bound,
gagged, and bludgeoned with a rock in his own workshop.

A gut-churning contradiction to a peaceful life.

Thirty-five years on, his murder remains unsolved
and the grand gladiolus beds are another's yard,
fenced off and grassy with sunny dots of dandelions.

A gardener had lived here and now he is gone,
but those who knew Hugh Chaffin remember
how he walked the rows and rows of dancing blooms.

Dignity is tortured,
murdered,
and dismembered.

Journalistic price:
speak out,
lose your life.

Machinations, disorder,
a farcical cover-up.

"Who saw him die?
I, said the fly."

Still, truth is denied,
the Crown Prince's
trapdoor of lies.
Pick one, Mr. President.

"America first!"

Not so, for a
Virginia resident
—by the name Jamal Khashoggi.

The Triops glides about his acrylic vivarium
Maybe a 300-million-year history enables
His seemingly carefree Snoopy dance
While on the other side of the tank
In a standard 6 by 8 internment, life is
Drifting to an inevitable, nondescript conclusion
Of my own making.

I set the controls for approval, burning
a lot of cosmic fuel just to say hello.

Talking used to come so easy; now
I pilot to the fringes to stay alive.

It would help if you liked Saul Bellow,
it would help if you knew Joy Harjo.

It would help if this capsule wasn't in deep
space, fading into the intergalactic void.

From his bedroom window, he sees
a poplar tree in the stronghold of a
thick, brown vine spiraling up its trunk.

He pours another ounce of brandy into his
morning cup of coffee and wonders if
the tree is fine with a slow demise too.

I pull back from enforced darkness as
yellow rays from the lantern skip on
cobblestones, the street is too quiet
now as I paint a reflective past of a
time and place where you walked as a
god across my terrace, into my cafe

Materializing before
Me
Claiming the twilight and brightening the night
Sitting, sipping the drink I took to
You
Lips on the edge of a perspiring glass
Eyes on the horizon, on everything and
nothing,
On mine.

And the night slipped away
Giving way to numbered days

When the sun shone on a smiling you
When your laughter shattered the odds
Before gravity's pull became apparent
Before our plans were ripped away.

I was thinking of you today, times past.

Alone (after Kyle J. Knapp)

Drunken,
Inconsolable,
Tired.
Every night
Muddled speech
Visions
And other graceless vexations.
Myself, trying to sleep
   One day
     I will.

Ouroboros
What's the fuss?
You swallowing me

Kick me down the hill
Drag you through the streets
Forgive us not our trespasses

John Wayne, yesterday's Duke,
was average on the draw
Like you, like me

Did we lend a helping hand?
Walk with Kings? Or forked memes,
with self-aggrandizing schemes

Ariana Grande has grown up
Since licking donuts for free
Likes her (4M), like me (—)

What goes around comes around
Mom used to say—it's just twisting
and daggering faster these days

Me swallowing you
What's the fuss?
Ouroboros

Meditating in the armchair one night
with the apartment lights down low.
Lee Morgan's up-tempo take on Cole Porter's
"Just One of Those Things" rocks the Bose
—jazz as lit as the day it was minted
A barn burner meeting the demands of my soul
as does the Jack Daniel's Tennessee Honey.
An ice cube melts, making that distinctive din
in my whiskey glass. (Old No. 7 heaven.)

I imagine Morgan's blistering licks breaking
it down and past that trapezoidal cube—
It's February 19, 1972, and Helen Morgan is pained
having been replaced with a new flame
then booted by Lee out of Slug's Saloon
into the bitter, unforgiving Manhattan night.
A pistol slides from her purse as if by providence.
She eyes the cold steel as snowflakes alight
on the metal barrel and quietly dissolve.

Helen takes the heat by the handle.

Walks back into the club.

She finds Lee and cuts him down
(that lost soul she had rescued years before)
with two shots to the chest. Lee's trumpet slips
from his grip before he crumbles in place.
She tosses the gun aside and cries out.

Bum-bah, bum-bah: the opening salvo
of "The Sidewinder" pulsates
bringing me back to the now.
Through the blinds, NYC illuminates the sky,
a vestige of where the Morgans had met
their hardscrabble end.

I raise my glass to their memory.

I leave them hanging,
nothing to say.
An inattentive friend,
nothing to do
with them.

Why not then,
erase limbs, body, head
—and scaffolding.
No more games.
I wish I may, I wish I might

But can't, truths
aren't welcome. So I don't answer
texts, return calls, and I leave
them on the gallows,
with nothing to say.

Familiar Quotations,
14th edition,1968—
a family hand me down
first owned
by a great uncle
who at the time
was leaving his wife
and two kids.

Of 1,750 pages
only one bears
a dog-eared corner,
one underline:

"The thought of suicide
is a great consolation:
by means of it one gets
successfully through
many a bad night."
— Nietzsche

An End of Sorts

Painted in a corner
late autumn
look at me go, nowhere

Sandpiper

I run along life's shore
dodging the cold spray
of those surfing
the same waves
of past slights,
real and reimagined,
until the storms
transform into tsunamis

These champion surfers
are charged by the
surge of drama,
never growing weary, and
I've become an accomplished
long-distance runner,
avoiding their heavy, wet sand
in my shoes.

Her eyes are open, yet she's not here,
I am sitting next to her,
staring at the end.

I've never been to Tyler until now
—a small, northeastern Texas town—
and will likely never be again.

But I came to be by her side
to hold Mom's hand as she lies
in a dolent hospice bed.

It's a stark, bitter scene
like a desolate border town from one
of the old, western TV shows
I'd watched as a kid, with her, long ago.
Except here in these rooms,
Alzheimer's is the ruthless gunslinger
—an unrelenting villain
armed with amyloid plaques—
and there's no hero-sheriff to save
the day when the wayward bullets
of this cold-blooded killer
strike down innocent bystanders.

Well-lit corridors, buffed and clean,
take the place of windswept, dusty streets.
And across the divide, glossy and pristine,
a six-shooter steals over the threshold,
heading straight for Mom's bed.
With a pivot and quick draw of the heel,

I smash the six-legged trespasser
into the hard, burnished tile ...
"Got it, Mom," I whisper,
feeling momentarily like a
much-needed paladin
in a surreal fray.

Her eyes are open, yet she's not here.
Perhaps she's reaching out
to a hand that's reaching back,
ready to catch the last train to the next frontier,
riding on through this night to a new dawn.

Still, at the end of every hard-earned day, people find some reason to believe. —*Bruce Springsteen*

While the great American whale is lost at sea
And the latest, edgy crime novel often dulls the fuck
out of me
I'll take some Dickinson, classic Emily,
The holy ghost of poetry.
And wade through her verses of trees, birds, and
ethereal beauty
... that always have a stamp of death for good measure.

Gauguin Night

Drifting off is a brutal
black and blue death roll
to the darkened deep,
over and over and over again,
and still no reprieve from   thinking.
She offers me her down-filled pillow
mistaken in her belief that the
feathery white softness will bring sleep,
but taking away her comfort
doesn't seem right.
So, I go to another room
and stretch out on the uncarpeted floor,
because when the mean reds hit
there's not much to do but ride 'em down.

On the iPad, I divert with a
Paul Gauguin documentary
where reality bends into illusion
on two-dimensional planes …
Innate strokes wrap
an innocent in sleep,
dreaming of birds
while bedside, a doll creeps.
Vivid colors amplify
the chrome yellow hues
of a forlorn Christ
on the cross, suffering anew.
Bold lines frame a raven
lurking near an open door—
a woman mourns a conception
lost … "nevermore."

Afterward, I head back to our room
with all that synthetist and primitive cool
running wild in my imagination and
dammit, to hell   I couldn't sleep.

The Need

A walking obsession,
creates fuel for the soul.
An itinerant biped at 7-10 miles a day
hints more than mere hobby.

The need is tripodal:
each step gets the blood flowing,
opens the basket to woolgather for writing,
and sets the bioclock for restful slumbering.

In straight hyperbole—
being ambulant keeps me alive.

She's a sunny day that loves the rain.

A chronic cold weighs me down,
spurring my astute, seven-year-old daughter
to gently coax me outside
into the garden,
saying the fresh air will do me good
—and it does.
But lifting the spirits more
is her crossing a magical transom …

Under a quaking aspen,
Ava pilots a toy hummingbird
low to the red wood chips,
then circles around a small hyacinth
hibernating in the autumn ground.
She whispers a dialect that exists before
liaisons with inanimates is lost.

I furtively behold,
unwilling to break the spell.
She broad-strokes the gray fall day in full color
with her fanciful, energetic flourishes;
and everything outside her realm falls away:
the job doesn't matter,
the bills don't matter, and
a world gone wrong trundles down.
This sole moment prevails,
and it is ours.

Ava crouches by the rock edging,
and reaches down.
A spider springs onto her hand

—a restrained shriek erupts.
No time passes before
she brushes it off with a heroic swipe,
then surges up and backs away.
I look for the eight-legged invader,
doing my best to allay her fears by
explaining Mother Nature's unexpected gifts
are part of the beauty all around us,
and well worth the occasional startle.

With order restored
my little charmer inches back to play,
the hummingbird returns to flight.

Later—
My reward for being her pillar,
a golden, heart-shaped leaf
that she found and gave to me.

I admire my wife's dedication to rearing our daughter.
Though we rightly assume in one ear and out the other,
still, the guiding motherly advice and the way it is told,
the kindness, or depending on the situation, strictness,
is a stamp that will be collected by the child who will forge
her own identity, cut from a priceless diamond.

Daughter

I write to leave for her—

a carefully crafted
house of words
for her to dwell
when my heart no longer beats

—an afterlife of words.

Alone
—first appeared at *Close to the Bone*, 10/30/2020

Before Gravity's Pull
—*Punk Noir Magazine*, 7/30/2021

Blue
—*Live Nude Poems*, 10/26/2021

Cri de Coeur
—*Punk Noir Magazine*, 10/26/2021

Dead Burying the Dead
—first appeared at *Close to the Bone*, 10/30/2020

Hangman
—*Punk Noir Magazine*, 11/12/2020

Holy Ghost of Poetry, The
—*Punk Noir Magazine*, 5/5/2021

Hugh Chaffin
—*The Five-2*, 2/3/2020

Inconsiderate, The
—*Live Nude Poems*, 7/31/2020

Killing of Jamal Khashoggi, The
— *BEAT to a PULP webzine*, 6/25/2019

Long Return, The
—*BEAT to a PULP webzine*, 6/25/2019

Lost in Space
—first appeared at *Close to the Bone*, 10/30/2020

No Line for a Common Thread
—*Punk Noir Magazine*, 4/7/2021

Sandpiper
—*Live Nude Poems*, 1/15/2021

Threads
—*Punk Noir Magazine*, 9/12/2021

Wherein, Demons
—first appeared at *Close to the Bone*, 10/30/2020

Whither Are We Drifting?
—*Punk Noir Magazine*, 11/12/2020

 David Cranmer's poems, short stories, articles, and essays have appeared in publications such as *Live Nude Poems*, *Needle: A Magazine of Noir*, *The Five-Two: Crime Poetry Weekly*, *LitReactor*, *Punk Noir Magazine*, Macmillan's *Criminal Element*, and *Chicken Soup for the Soul*. He's a dedicated Whovian who enjoys jazz and backgammon. He can be found in scenic upstate New York where he lives with his wife and daughter.

Made in the USA
Middletown, DE
05 May 2022

65301162R00035